D0498087

# A Fury of Motion

# A Fury of Motion

## Poems for Boys

### Charles Ghigna

Foreword by X. J. Kennedy

Wordsong
☆
Boyds Mills Press

# Acknowledgments

The author gratefully acknowledges the editors and publishers of the following magazines in which some of these poems first appeared. All poems are copyright Charles Ghigna.

"Air Force," *Writer's Digest*, March 1989; "*Ars Longa, Vita Brevis*," *The Artist's Magazine*, October 1991; "Art," *The Artist's Magazine*, April 1993; "Balloon Man," *Storyworks*/Scholastic, April 1997; "The Bowman's Hand," *English Journal*, December 1993; "Chess Nut," *Chess Life*, March 1994; "Family Tree," *Children's Digest*, February 1987; "The Firefly," *Children's Digest*, July 1996; "Headway," *Guideposts*, March 1994; "Hunting Boys," *Birmingham Magazine*, October 1993; "Inspiration," *Writer's Digest*, April 1984; "The Porcupine Poem," *Writer's Digest*, June 1998; "Racing the Wind," *Storyworks*/Scholastic, April 1997; "School-Yard Showdown," *Florida Magazine, Orlando Sentinel*, March 1975; "Science Faction," *Highlights for Children*, September 1991; "Snowfall in the City," *Cricket*, January 1995; "Tell Me," *Writer's Digest*, April 1985 and March 1989; "Writer's Block," *Writer's Digest*, January 1995.

Copyright © 2003 by Charles Ghigna • All rights reserved

Published by *Wordsong* • Boyds Mills Press, Inc. • A Highlights Company
815 Church Street • Honesdale, Pennsylvania 18431
Printed in China through Colorcraft Ltd., Hong Kong

Publisher Cataloging-in-Publication Data (U.S.)

Ghigna, Charles.
A fury of motion : poems for boys / Charles Ghigna ;
foreword by X. J. Kennedy.—1st ed. • [64] p.   cm.
Summary: Poems about sports, family, school, etc.
ISBN 1-59078-066-3 • ISBN 1-59078-188-0 (pbk).
1. Children's poetry, American. 2. Boys—Juvenile poetry.
(1. American poetry. 2. Boys—Poetry.) I. Kennedy, X. J. II. Title.
811/ .54  21 • PS3602.I242  2003 • 2003101692

First edition, 2003
The text of this book is set in 12-point Minion.
Visit our Web site at www.boydsmillspress.com

10 9 8 7 6 5 4 3 2   hc
10 9 8 7 6 5 4 3 2 1 pbk

To my son, Chip,
for giving me more than one reason to write

To Richard Armour, in memoriam,
for making me read "Armour's Armory"
before the sports page

And to X. J. Kennedy
for keeping me out of the dugout

—C. G.

# Contents

# Foreword

**D**oes poetry annoy you? Have you ever wondered what good it is, whether it's for you? If you answer yes to any of those questions, then I'm on your side. I've been there myself. So has Charles Ghigna (rhymes with KEEN-ya), who wrote this surprising book.

Back in the sixth grade, I didn't actually hate poetry, but I did distrust the stuff. Oh, in my earlier years I'd met some Mother Goose jingles, and they'd been easy to swallow. Some were simple, little-kid stuff. Others were spooky and mysterious—like this:

> *Hinx! Minx! The old witch winks!*
> *The fat begins to fry.*
> *There's nobody home*
> *But Jumping Joan,*
> *Jumping Joan and I!*

I didn't know who Jumping Joan was, but this silly little poem told a Halloweeny kind of story. It gave the impression that that wicked witch knew some horrible secret. And whose fat was she frying—Hansel's and Gretel's?

Later on in my young life, my mother had read me some verse by Robert Louis Stevenson about taking a ride on a swing—

> *Up in the air and over the wall,*
> *Till I can see so wide,*
> *Rivers and trees and cattle and all*
> *Over the countryside . . .*

I loved to swing, and so Stevenson's poem talked to me. Besides, it had a nice bouncy beat to it.

But in sixth grade, poetry suddenly became awful. We had to read a long, long poem by Henry Wadsworth Longfellow about some lady named Evangeline who got lost in the woods, or something. I couldn't get interested. Every night, when I had to read a few pages of it, I felt like somebody eating his way through a haystack. Years later, I actually came to like some poems of Longfellow's, but at the time, that slow-moving poem didn't appeal to me. I didn't much like any of the other poems the teacher liked, either. She seemed to believe that all the poets worth reading had died fifty or more years ago.

By and by, when I reached high school, I discovered that not all poetry put me off. Some of it was even written by people who were still alive. But that's another story, and already I've blabbed too much about myself. All I'm trying to do is to assure you that, if you don't care for poetry, you aren't alone. And that there's nothing the matter with you.

So here's Charles Ghigna trying to give you a bunch of poems you'll like. Why don't you give his book a try? What can you lose except a little time that you might otherwise spend watching television commercials? And maybe—just maybe—you'll find, as I did, that poetry is fun, at least some of it. You see, Ghigna writes about some things you just might care about. In this book, you'll learn what it's like to be a shortstop making a sensational double play, what it's like to be a skydiver with the wind screaming past your ears. Some poems are short and funny (like "Lunchroom Magic"). A few are sad. A few will give you (as Ghigna puts it) "a glimpse of who you are."

Maybe you won't care for every one of Ghigna's poems. OK, but suppose you find a few that really talk to you. Suppose you even find yourself tucking away a poem in the back of your memory. Then whenever you're bored, waiting for a bus or for a movie to start, you can remember the poem and silently say it to yourself, and let it entertain you all over again.

By the way, as a poet Charles Ghigna has a terrific track record. He's written several fine books for young readers and adults, and some have proved quite popular.

Read this book, and the next time you meet poetry, maybe you won't run away. Maybe you'll say, "Come on, poems! Do your worst! Show me your best! I'm not scared of you."

One last note—to any girls who might have wandered into this all-boy party: There isn't any law against your reading these poems. Some of them, I think, could appeal to anybody. Reading certain ones will be like looking at the world through a boy's glasses. Who knows what secrets you might find out?

—X. J. Kennedy

# Introduction

When I was your age, I hated poetry. I thought it was for sissies and grandmothers, and I didn't want any part of it.

I played on my high-school baseball team and wanted to be a major-league player when I grew up. I played American Legion baseball and tried out with the Pittsburgh Pirates more than thirty years ago.

I'm still waiting to hear from them.

The first poem I ever wrote was for a girl in school. I liked her a lot, but she didn't even know I existed.

The teacher found it and made me read it in front of the class. I thought I was going to die. After school, the girl told me she liked my poem and gave me a kiss on the cheek.

I've been writing poems ever since.

Hope you enjoy some of these.

—— C. G

# Shortstop

The slits of his eyes
hidden in shadows
beneath the bill of his cap,
he watches and waits
like a patient cat
to catch what comes
his way.

*Crack!*
and he pounces
upon the ball,
his hands flying
above the grass,
flinging his prey
on its way
across the diamond
into a double play.

# Baseball Dreams

*In memory of Jack Marsh,*
*second baseman, Yale University, 1943*


Before the bayonet replaced the bat,
Jack Marsh played second base for Yale,
his spikes anchored into the August clay,
his eyes set deep against the setting sun.

The scouts all knew his numbers well,
had studied his sure hands that flew
like hungry gulls above the grass;
but Uncle Sam had scouted, too,

had chosen first the team to play
the season's final game of '44,
had issued him another uniform
to wear into the face of winter moon

that shone upon a snowy plain,
where players played a deadly game,
where strikes were thrown with each grenade,
and high-pitched echoes linger still.

Beyond the burned-out foreign fields
and boyhood dreams of bunts and steals,
young Jack Marsh is rounding third
and sliding, sliding safely home.

# Football

Sweat
Mud
Dirt
Blood

Snow
Rain
Fear
Pain

Win
Yell
Lose
Hell

# Tackle

A grizzly bear in shoulder pads,
he growls at the line of scrimmage,
snarls into the face of the offense,
and glares into the eyes
of the opposing quarterback.

Hike!
and he explodes
over the line,
bursts through
the whirling blitz
of cracking helmets,
his legs churning forward
in a fury of motion,
his arms flailing
through the backfield
for anything that moves.

# Basketball Tryout

The All-State boy from Alabama
faked, leaped, drifted, and shot
for the New England coach
and his dollar cigar.
A scholarship, apartment, new car,
and a name rode on his midair act.
But the ball and the boy were buddies,
and again his try was good.
Without missing a beat,
he took the one-bounce rebound,
spun into a lay-up, grabbed it
coming through the strings,
raced low to the opposite court,
faked, leaped, drifted, and shot.
Again the strings played his song.

On a silent count of three,
the one-man audience
pulled the unpuffed cigar from his mouth,
his silver-dollar eyes
already on the championship.
"Where'd ja learn that stuff?"
The All-State boy from Alabama
spun, dipped, jumped, and said,
"High school."
Through the boy's thick drawl
and the gym's hollow acoustics,
the coach misheard it as "I'ze cool."
Pale, he called the boy "boy,"
preceded it with "hey,"
and followed it up with
"that's all."

# Soccer

The long kick comes
and out of the pack
the midfielder rises,

his eyes on the ball,
his forehead set like a fist
ready to punch it home.

# Tennis Lion

Perfect circles useless here,
I take off my watch
before each match
and let my pulse run wild.

Entering the court,
I pace the foul line for luck
and stare across the net
at my prey.

I am a lion.
This is my open cage.

# Boxing Lesson

Each champion must realize
When he is in his prime
That no one's ever won a bout
Against the hands of time.

# Hunting Boys

It happens every year
from autumn to spring—
a dozen or so are lost,
good ole boys, every one:
boys from Butler County,
Bibb, Clarke, and Cullman,
boys from Bullock and Clay,
boys who stay up late
every November evening
rubbing oil and dreams
into the steel of old guns,
boys who leave warm homes
to walk cold woods, forever.

# Skydiver

First step
and he swallows
the dry, delicious fear
of walking on air.

Body bent back
into a bow,
he falls into the arms
of the screaming wind,
his heart beating
taps in his ears.

*Pop,*
and an angel wing
pulls him from the thunder
of a hundred-
mile-an-hour dream.

He sits perched,
a runaway cloud
of contentment,
a fearless eagle feather
lost in the drift
of an early afternoon.

Knees bent, he pulls
the taut reins of reality,
ready-sets himself
for one final, little lift,
one last tiptoe of air
before his flying feet
must run their
earthbound way
back home.

# Science Faction

Nature, it's true,
Is full of surprises:
The sun doesn't set,
The horizon rises.

# Ants Never Cry "Uncle"

Consider the little ant.
He never says, "I can't."
And so it comes as no surprise,
He carries things ten times his size.

# April Sideshow

Like a magnet
under the magician's table,
the swan's reflection
pulls her across the lake,
while deep inside the brush
an unseen hand pulls rabbits
out of rabbits.

# Balloon Man

He sells his breath
in shiny rubber bags.
They call him concession-

aire.

# Air Force

Do not think only of planes in combat,
of military pride and might.
Think of that gentle force of air,

that breath of boyhood magic
that turns candles into wishes
and balloons into birthdays,

that unseen breeze that spins
pinwheels and pushes sailboats,
that teaches toy horns to toot,

that fills each inner tube
and rubber raft with laughter,
that holds up every kite

like a child's heart
and lets it soar higher
than an endless summer sky.

# Racing the Wind

I like to ride on my bike every day
Where the limbs of trees
Shake hands in the breeze
Over my head with the tips of their leaves.

I like to race with the sun in my face
Down trails I know
Where no one goes
Except the wind that blows and blows.

# The Beach

Hush.
Watch your step.
Eternity is here,

finely ground shells
holding forth
against the roar of time.

# Evening Parade

A summer storm
Stirs my slumber
As clouds march by
To claps of thunder.

# The Firefly

The firefly is quite a sight
Upon the summer wind.
Instead of shining where he goes,
He lights up where he's been.

# Orion

August night,
and the stars
gather
like moths
around
the rising
lantern
of moon.

# Autumn's Way

In their yellow-most goings,
leaves of maple
ride breezes to the ground.
You can hear their sound
each autumn afternoon
as the crisp air cuts
through the trees
and hurries us along
the golden sidewalks
home.

# Snowfall
# in the City

Covered in creamy
birthday-cake frosting,
the parked cars
huddle beneath
their streetlamp candles,
waiting for the North Wind
to come make its wish
for morning.

# Family Tree

My roots are deep within you,
Growing as you grow.
My shade provides the shelter
For the new seeds that you sow.

No matter what the season,
I stand here still the same.
Come winter, spring, or summer,
My branches bear your name.

# I Wish I Had a Twin

I wish I had a brother twin
Who looked like me and I like him.
Every day we'd have such fun
Being two who looked like one.

# Father Time

Third grade,
and I am onstage in a toga
playing Father Time,

a staff in my hand,
a beard of cotton
under my chin,

my friends
at my feet
staring up at me.

Suddenly
I am older
than everyone,

older than
my older sisters,
older than

my parents,
older than
my teacher,

who told me
I would one day
remember the line

I forgot
when I played
Father Time.

# Loco Motion

Time, a runaway train,
races through
the tunnel vision of our future

while we sit and stare
at the mirrored windows
of our past.

# Chess Nut

There's nothing like a game of chess.
It's patience at its height;
Where else can you just sit and take
All day to move one knight?

# School

Class
Girls
New
Worlds

Sports
Stars
Fast
Cars

Grades
Test
No
Rest

# School Daze

From algebra to English class,
I've lost my mind, I swear;
One teacher says that pie is round,
The other—pie are square!

# Lunchroom Magic

Of all the magic I have seen
My favorite, I suppose,
Was yesterday at lunch when Mark
Made milk come out his nose.

# School-Yard Showdown

The boy with cocked hips,
a hand on one,
holds with his words
a giggle of girls behind him.

They do not hear
the trace of quakes
in his voice that he feels
coming through on the bones of boyhood.

In front of this almost-man
stands another boy
with hands on cocked hips,
holding his own little giggle of girls.

They talk big to each other
and try to stand bigger,
each hoping the other won't move.

They hide inside their words,
wishing a fist will fly from their hip
and somehow make them a man.

# The Bowman's Hand

*"A fifteen-year-old athlete died of cardiac arrest from a high-school
friend's punch in the chest during a classroom 'cuss game' popular with
students. Witnesses said he complimented his opponent on the 'good hit,'
then died."*

—The Birmingham News

The game over, the target rests on the ground;
but the heavy hand of the standing boy
will carry the weight of this dark moment

into the bull's-eye of memory, into the
corners of every swollen night.
This is the hand that will open and close

too many times before it sleeps,
before it catches that first star,
shines it bright within its praying palm,

puts it back into the black heaven of boyhood.
This is the hand that will shade the eyes
that study the sky for a cloudless past,

the hand that will grip and hold
the burning weight of growing old.
This is the hand that will not rest in peace,

that will not heal the broken arrow,
that will not lose its quiver;
the hand that will shake inside

the hand of too many smiling strangers.
This is the hand that will caress a sleeping son
named after his father's brave young friend,

after the one untouched by time,
untouched by the sharpness of age,
by the point of a pointless game.

# Tell Me

about how you lost
your interest
in words,

about how you feel
so full
of them

you think you might
break out
in red letters,

think if you hear
another one
you will scream,

will run blindly
into the woods
and hide,

will dip your finger
into the stream
and write your final line,

will lie on your back
and stare up
at the stars,

will run home
through the dark
and sit alone by the fire

until someone who cares
comes to your side and says,
"Tell me."

# The Leopard
# of Loneliness

Loneliness, the leopard,
Stalks the heart;
He captures his prey
And tears it apart.

When he is through,
He goes for the bone;
When he is full,
He leaves you—alone.

# Trip

I'm going on vacation in my mind.
I'm going there to see what I might find.
If I'm not back by half past eight,
Please don't stay. Please don't wait.

Please don't call. Please don't write.
I'm going, going out of sight.
Please don't cry and carry on.
I'm going, going, going—gone.

# Dreamland

Each night we leave this world of ours
And venture out past shooting stars
Into a world beyond our bed—
The universe inside our head.

# Ars Longa, Vita Brevis
## (Art Is Long, Life Is Short)

Like the sculptor
who chips away
at what is not
the sculpture,
your life
is in your hands,
the pure
imperfect stone
waiting for its
daily touch,
the gentle tap,
the savored strike
toward mass
and space
that form
the perfect past,
your tribute
to the art
of living.

# In Sight

Close your eyes and look inside,
A mirror shines within;
To find where you are going,
First see where you have been.

# Headway

Do not let fear confine your life
Inside a shell of doubt;
A turtle never moves until
His head is sticking out.

# Over Herd

This time it will be different.
This time we will not go
like our bovine brothers

one by one down the ramp,
headfirst through the chute
into the slaughterhouse,

into the waiting slug of night.
This time we will rouse the herd,
we will rise from our dung-

drenched funeral boards,
we will sway from side to side
in our heavy wave of defiance,

we will dance our rite to life,
we will rock and roll this cattle car
right off its clacking tracks.

# Haircut

Sit still on the eye-seat
in a room full of mirrors
while the pink-palmed man

dressed in white breathes
down your clean-shaven neck
and some scissors click out

a cold tune to an old song
about wrestling, war,
or the weather.

Step down from your chair
of instant conformity,
trod upon the hair-grass to the door;

let this be the last time
you pay for giving of your
self.

# Inspiration

It is everything
you think it is.
It is the end
of the tunnel
and the light
up ahead.
It is the sound
of the wind
and the silence
of the night.
It is the sun
and the moon
and the memory.
It is the eye
and the hand
and the mouth.
It is the present
and the future
and the past.
It is here.
It is there.
It is gone.

# Art

Art is undefinable,
A mystery of creation
Inspired by a pigment
Of your imagination.

# Writer's Block

The path to inspiration starts
Upon the trails we've known;
Each writer's block is not a rock,
But just a stepping stone.

# The Porcupine Poem

*Porcupines can raise their quills, turn around, and run
backward into their prey.*

Just when you think
you are done with it,
the poem turns on you,

charges back for more,
pricks you with its
finer points,

reminds you
things are not
what they seem,

that the past is not past
until it turns and shows
its sharp, uncompromising side.

# What's a Poem?

A whisper,
a shout,
thoughts turned
inside out.

A laugh,
a sigh,
an echo
passing by.

A rhythm,
a rhyme,
a moment
caught in time.

A moon,
a star,
a glimpse
of who you are.